Life's Reflection

Liela Marie Fuller

Jadora's Child Publishing
Middletown, Connecticut

All rights reserved. Absolutely no part of this book may be reproduced, stored in or introduced into any retrieval system, or transmitted in any form or by any means without the expressed written consent of the Publisher or the Author of this book.

Copyright © 2005 Liela Marie Fuller

Cover Design: MERK Media
Editor: Kallie Falandays (telltellpoetry.com)

Library of Congress Catalog Number: 2013455100

ISBN-10:0996128905
ISBN-13:978-0-9961289-0-2

Second Edition

Critical Acclaim for Life's Reflection

In this compilation of poetry, Author Liela Fuller has given us a glimpse of her reflections on the challenges, triumphs and experiences that we seldom bring to light. Liela's poems connect us with that which we feel but don't often express. She has given voice to the voiceless, hope and encouragement to the disheartened and inspiration to us all. I look forward to seeing more of her work.

Gladys Anderson

Author of Master the Genie Within: Uncover, Embrace and Celebrate the Real You.

I feel as though I have been privileged to be invited along on the short tour of Fuller's life. I especially loved the Expose of a Black Woman and appreciate her evident self-love. Fuller is an example for all young Black women. I would like to see this as required reading in New Jersey. My second most favorite part was that of her son, Malachi. There is no truer love than that of a mother for her precious son; he is her shining star. Beautiful, a must read.

Jackie Saulmon Ramirez

Great work from a great author! Real and raw . . . Life in artistry. Looking forward to her next work. Life's reflection puts you in a place of introspection and motivates you to live your best life!

Anita Hodge

This book was a combination of emotions that were from deep down in the Author's heart and soul...Amazing use of descriptive language...everyone could relate to one or more of the chapters...Can't say enough about how much I enjoyed it - get them for all the women in your family - they will love them.

Dotti Taylor

The first poem in this collection was very powerful and was followed by another that left me with an arched brow and a satisfied smile. Liela Marie Fuller was very crafty with those pieces and from the beginning, I couldn't wait to see what else the poet had in store. In "Life's Reflection," Fuller expounds upon relationships, whether it be between a male and female, Creator and creation, or a mother and child. She reminds her audience that women are queens and men are kings. There is an abundance of love-centered poetry that many should be able to relate to. I look forward to seeing Fuller grow and produce more work as a poetic writer.

OOSA Online Book Club

Contents

ABUSED AND OBSESSED 1

THE RAPE CONTINUES..3

THE HARLOT...THAT'S MY NAME 5

IS LOVE WHAT YOU CALL IT 7

OBSESSED..10

OBSESSED PT.2 12

HEARTACHE AND PAIN 15

TRAGEDY 16

I'M SORRY 17

FROM FANTASY TO REALITY 18

TRAPPED 19

TEARS 20

HEART BREAK 21

BLACK ROSE..22

ALL THAT I CAN DO 24

THE EXPRESSION OF SHE 26

EXPOSÉ OF A BLACK WOMAN..27

LIFELESS REFLECTION IN CHANGING CIRCUMSTANCE 29

I AM BLACK WOMAN...30

WHAT DO YOU SEE WHEN YOU LOOK AT ME? 32

THIS IS FORCED...34

IN HIS SERVICE..37

DIFFERENT ME..38

RUNNING FOR MY LIFE	40
THE CALL	42
THE WONDROUS ONE	44
THE MANNER OF HIS LOVE	46
FALLING IN LOVE WITH MY FATHER	47
A LOVE STORY	48
ADDICTED	50
TO MY LOVE…	52
THANK YOU FOR LOVING ME	54
TO MY KING WITH LOVE	55
WILL YOU LOVE ME?	56
FOR MALACHI	58
THE VOWS (FOR MY HUSBAND)	59
THE EVOLUTION OF QUEEN	60
SOME DAYS	62
YOUR TOUCH IS ALL I NEED	64
AS LONG AS I AM QUEEN	66
YES, I DO LOVE YOU	67
LOVE SOUP	69
TRUTH IS…	70
FOR MY WEDDING DAY	72
YOU SHOULD HAVE	73
ONCE UPON A LOVE TIME	75
THINKING OF YOU	77
IT MAKES NO GOOD SENSE	78
JUST BETWEEN YOU AND ME	79

COLD NIGHTS	80
FOR MY LOVE	81
SWEET THANG...I ADORE YOU	82
WHY I LEFT JAZZ	83
BEHOLDING THE BEAUTY	85
AND MY MIND WONDERS	87
MISSING YOU BUT NOT REALLY TRYING	88
TO JOHNNY WALKER RED	89
EASIER SAID THAN DONE	90
DISTANT FRIEND	91
I LOVE YOU	93
VOICE OF THE QUEEN	94
THE MOTHER IN ME	96
I HAVE TRIED TO SAVE YOU	97
I SEE IN YOU	98
WISHES AND DREAMS	99
FOR MY MOTHERS	100
SISTER 2 SISTER	101
I REMEMBER WHO YOU USED TO BE (FOR CAMDEN, NJ)	104

DEDICATION

To my son Malachi – You are truly a blessing and an awesome young man. I am proud of who you are and I am patiently waiting to see the great man I know you will become. I love you!

ACKNOWLEDGMENTS

I would like to thank my Lord and Savior Jesus Christ – without Him, this would not have been possible. To God be the Glory!

For Janet and Dorothy – your love made this possible and I know you're in Heaven smiling on me. You are why Jadora's Child exists!

For my parents – thank you for all of your support. I love you.

Mrs. Linda Dominique Grosvenor-Holland – thank you for mentoring me. Your advice and input have proven invaluable! You are an awesome kingdom blessing! May blessings ABOUND in your account!

For all those who read and believed – thank you for your belief in me. There were days when I needed your faith to stand on and you provided it. You will never know how much it meant to me. Blessings!

ABUSED AND OBSESSED

THE RAPE CONTINUES...

Stop!

Don't!

Please Stop!

You know you want it.

Stop!

Shut up or I'll kill you...you said as you pushed me down on the bed I had made with another.

You came into my home

And you terrorized my life.

I said no, so why didn't you stop?

I said please don't, so why did you continue?

I laid there while your hand found places I didn't want you to know.

I laid there while you kissed me as though it was something I wanted.

I laid there as you placed your so-called manhood inside of me, ripping away my trust, my self-worth, and my self-esteem.

You rode me as if I were a champion horse.

You moaned as if I were the best you had ever had.

BUT I SAID NO!

I never wanted this...I never wanted you!

BUT YOU FORCED YOURSELF INSIDE ME!

I laid there and tried to imagine that this was a dream but the more I smelled the stink of your sweat, the more I realized it was not a dream and tears fell from my face.

You laid your body on me and I was helpless.

I never wanted this…

I SAID NO,

But you took a piece of me.

Don't call the police or I'll be back!

If I had a gun, I'd shoot you. God would forgive me, He'd have to, I thought, because I would have just cause!

I never called 911. I never wanted anyone to know.

But you left more of you than I imagined.

You left your seed in me.

You left me with your baby.

And when I look at your child's face, the rape continues.

THE HARLOT...THAT'S MY NAME

Harlot, Working Girl, Prostitute: I've been called all
these, but I am just like any other woman you see.

I've got goals and dreams. I've got more to offer
than what you see. There is so much more I'd rather be.

But that's not what you see...
You came to see my work, right?

You came to see how good this trick could be?
See, I know all about you.

I may not know your name,
but I sure 'nuf know your game.

You are looking for a quick fix
for your sexual inhibitions.

You want me to please you in that dirty perverted way
that your woman can't.

You don't want to know about me because to you,
I am nothing but a quickie.

That's all you want— a real good blow and lay,
but I've got more to offer this life than that.

Yes, I am a harlot now but that's not where I want to be.
I've got goals and dreams;

I want to get out of this life but I don't know how.
I don't want to be on my back all my life, but I am
doomed to live this way, because it's a part of me. A part

of my being, and no matter what I do,
the harlot is me.

She is my other self—the other woman I can't get rid of.
She has taken me places I never wanted to go.

She has taken me to depths that I did not think possible,
yet I dwell with her in disgusting depths and vile venues

to get the fix of sexual peaks. She took my goals
and dreams and buried them deep away from me but I
remember that this is not who I was destined to be.

I remember that I had goals and dreams.
I remember the life she stole from me.

I wanted a better life, but the harlot claimed my
existence as her own.

She's held me captive in this life
and while I am trying to break free,

I feel there is no way to truly be *just me* again,
because, you see, she is me, and I am her…

The harlot & me.

IS LOVE WHAT YOU CALL IT

I wanted you to touch me today.

I wanted your arms wrapped around my waist.

I wanted to feel you close to me.

I wanted you here, but the reality came flooding back.

I remember your hands wrapped around my neck,

Hurting me. Choking me.

I remember how you squeezed my arm until my brown skin bruised purple.

I remember all the times you said you loved me...

Is this what you meant?

Is this what love feels like?

Is love supposed to hurt this way?

I remember you saying I'm sorry.

I remember thinking how dumb I was to let you back in.

How dare you put your hands on ME that way?

The hands that were supposed to nurture me.

The hands that were supposed to take care of me; hands that were supposed to love me.

I remember the noise your hand made against my face.

Smack!

I remember the sight of your fist hitting my eye.

"Please don't," I cried.

I remember our children running to my side.

"Daddy, please don't hurt mommy!"

I remember the lies I told those who asked, "Is he beating you?"

"No," I would say — "I fell from the chair."

I remember momma looking at my swollen eye and lip

"I don't believe you," she cried.

I remember letting you back into our home.

Hoping we'd make it, but deep down knowing we had already failed.

What would our friends think?

They admired us in the light, never knowing who we became in the dark.

I remember letting you in that last time.

As I opened the door to you, I silently prayed that we would work this out.

I remember your fists on my face.

I remember feeling my chest caving in from the punches you threw.

I remember my body coasting through the glass pane in our living room.

The children screaming and pleading with you to leave me alone.

Your eyes glossed and my eyes closed.

Sirens…Ambulance…Police

In the distance, I could hear momma screaming, "You killed my baby, you bastard!"

"Where am I?" I cried

God answered, "All is well now, daughter. Rest."

OBSESSED

You read my books, yet you hate me.

You looked at my life and tried to recreate me.

You wanted to become me and make my life your own.

You had me in your sights from the day my book hit the stands.

You violated my life and my soul.

Your obsession was destined to destroy me.

You broke into my place and violated my home.

You rifled through my belongings and robbed my house of its home.

As I opened the door to my home, there you were—obsessed.

I turned on the lights.

Flash!

"Who are you? Why are you here?" I said

"I'm your number one fan."

"Please leave."

"God told me that you are mine! You belong to me!"

I reached for the cell in my pocket.

I pressed the numbers I had rehearsed, knowing that my fame would bring this day.

I pressed send.

"Listen, why are doing this? Why are you in my house?"

Through my earpiece, my security says they're on their way.

"Please leave."

I saw the gun and I raised my hands.

"Please don't shoot me…this is not how you want me!"

"If I can't have you then no one can!"

Through my earpiece, my security says they're making their way to the stairs and my heart hoped they'd make it.

"Quietly."

"What did you say?"

"Just do it quietly."

I knelt and it startled you.

I heard the footsteps I had been trained to hear.

The doors opened and you were arrested,

Yet I am still affected.

I feel displaced in my space.

Is this the price to this life?

How can I live if I can't live free?

OBSESSED PT.2

It's 7 a.m. and I am dressing for your trial.

I've looked over my shoulder a thousand times.

Part of me is waiting.

Part of me is scared.

I sit in the front row.

I stand as the judge comes in.

You get 6 months on a deal.

"What the hell?"

"I am ordering the Defendant to stay 500 feet away from his victim at all times."

Does this judge realize that he can stand 500 feet away and still shoot me?

I get up— frustrated at this system that is supposed to protect me.

I am aggravated at this judge who should be shielding me.

Cameras flash as I rush out surrounded by security.

"Queen! Queen! What will you do now?"

"Protect myself since the system can't."

I leave knowing that my fame has brought me here.

My dreams are realized, but my nightmare has just

begun.

Today, my security gets tighter and
My life becomes less mine.

Tomorrow, the gates go up around my estate.
I'm having my orange jumpsuit custom made.

I'm living the American Dream.
I'm also living the American Nightmare.

I am a prisoner of my fame;
I am celebrity-media made.

HEARTACHE AND PAIN

"Love has not always been easy for me but every loss has lead me right to where I was supposed to be."

~ Liela

TRAGEDY

Your hand…My hand…They touched…We were once one and now you are gone from me.

You are gone and I am left to battle the world alone.

When I lost you, I lost my best friend.

You were the one who listened and never judged.

When I lost you, I lost my guide and compass.

I no longer have a well-devised plan.

Everything that I once knew seems a distance memory now that you are gone from me.

I have lost part of my past, my present, and my future.

You were a timeless treasure that, like a great antique, I thought would last forever, but now you are gone and I feel adrift without you.

You were my inspiration and now I aspire to remember you.

I am your hopes, dreams, and wishes living in this generation.

You are no longer a body with a name, but a Spirit watching closely over me.

Watch me now as I soar past the valleys and over the mountain tops to success.

I'M SORRY

I did it.

I did all the things I said I would never do.

I tried to change. I tried to be the one you wanted.

I tried to be better. Tried to live better. I tried to do better, but I messed up.

I'm sorry.

Even though what I did was not a crime, I know I must do my time.

I'm sorry that I hurt you and put our love on the line.

I hate what I did to you.

I dislike who we've become because of my lie.

I'm sorry that this apology can't take away the pain.

I'm sorry that this apology can't change the fears you have about me.

I'm sorry that this apology can't transform us back to the past where I knew the future.

I'm sorry…I know that it doesn't mean much…I can't take it away but I'm sorry is all that I can say.

I wish I could turn back and make the right choice, but, my love, I can't.

I'm sorry… I know it can never be enough, but I'm sorry.

I'm sorry is all that I can say.

FROM FANTASY TO REALITY

It's been heart-wrenching days and sleepless nights since we ended.

I understand why it happened, but my heart still longs for you.

It's so hard not to pick up the phone and dial your number.

All I want to do is hear you say you love me.

I find myself dreaming that yours is the hand that will save me from falling, but then you let go.

I don't know what to do anymore.

 I don't know where to go.

I can't find my ground.

I no longer have a safety net. There is nothing to hold me and no one to protect me.

All my dreams have been ripped from my heart; my love has been snatched away.

I am unhappy without you; I no longer want this life.

My joy has been stolen from me.

I don't want another love! I can't move on!

You became my King. No, you can't resign your crown.

I want you back here in my reality.

TRAPPED

Trapped…that's the way I feel lying alone—

Trapped in a heart that's longing for another,

Trapped in friendships that have no meaning,

Surrounded by men who only want one thing.

Trapped in a stressful place needing you to come for me.

I feel trapped wanting you to hold me in your arms but knowing you'll deny me,

Trapped by the love I feel for you and the love you will not hear of—

The love you will not accept,

The love that obsessed me with you --

The love that has gone from my heart and come back as sadness—

I feel trapped in my life waiting for you to come to me and set me free.

TEARS

Today you gave me a part of you and I gave you a part of me but now the tears are falling from my eyes.

It was not easy to come here and do this with you and maybe you need to know the truth, but I am so afraid.

Afraid that the truth will halt this thing that we have just begun,

So the tears continue to fall and I continue to wonder…

Wonder if I tell you, how you will feel; how you will react.

Wonder if I will ever see you again once I say my peace.

Wonder if this will be the end — if you knew the secret that lies in my smile.

And the tears keep falling.

HEART BREAK

I want to get out of this hell I feel in my heart but you stand in the way blocking the door.

I want your hands to heal the heartache that surrounds me, but you won't touch me.

I want to feel you surrounding me, enveloping me, making me a part of you but you stand there with arms folded. You're trying to defy love.

I want you to overtake me, captivate me, make me scream your name, but there you sit not wanting me like I want you.

I want to hold your love in my hand and have you with me, but you stand there blocking your heart from loving me.

And my heart breaks because all I've ever wanted was your love.

BLACK ROSE

Ode to you black rose; you who spring up in my secret place.

You sit in the midst of the abyss,

Watching me,

Waiting for me.

You grow in my trials and thrive in my circumstance.

You deliver my ruin.

Your thorns are long and hard—

They prick my spirit and decimate my self-esteem.

Your petals are firm like concrete and your weeds choke the life from me.

Your stem steps on the bane of my existence.

Your weight— like bricks holding back my stride.

Black rose, you destroy the soil of my secret garden.

I thought I could kill you by depriving you, yet you still grow.

Wickedly, you take out all that is around you. I thought I'd rid you by walking the other way, yet my feet sink into the abyss.

You zap the nutrients from my seed and you grow.

You make living in your midst indescribable.

Yet I will conquer you.

Although you are strong, I will be stronger.

Black rose, you will be picked and obliterated for sanity's sake.

ALL THAT I CAN DO

It's been all that I can do to hold back the tears.

It's been all that I can do just to get over you.

It's been all that I can do to remember your smile.

It's been all that I can do to keep you in my heart.

It's been all that I can do just to bring myself back to this life without you.

It's been all that I can do to keep myself from dying inside.

It's been all that I can do to remember your sweet face.

It's been so long and the one thing I will never do is stop loving you.

THE EXPRESSION OF SHE

"I love me some Me! It took me a long time to get here but I really love me ~ Every part of me! I love every piece of me! And that's God because He made all of me!"
~ Liela

EXPOSÉ OF A BLACK WOMAN

I have decided to love me—

Not just some of me, but all of me!

I have decided to look at me—

Not just some of me, but all of me!

I am beautiful—wonderfully made from the inside out.

I love all of me.

I love my breasts—

    Full and standing at attention

I love my hips

    As they sway from right to left.

I love my lips…

    Sexy and perfect.

I love the curves in my jeans

    Because big or small, everyone is looking.

I love my hands…

    In them I hold love and experience.

I love my eyes…

    They show the true Diva inside.

I love my hair…

    Because good or bad, straight or nappy, it's my heritage.

I love my face…

> For it brings all of my beauty inside and out to you.

Perfect, I'm not, but beautiful…that's me!

LIFELESS REFLECTION IN CHANGING CIRCUMSTANCE

I started this journey hoping that it would end the confusion in my head.

I hoped that it would answer all the questions that I had.

I wanted it to prove something, not just to me but to those who knew that, for once, my journey was on course.

Yet when I look over this time, I see a reflection of me.

Really it's who I used to be…bottled up and confused.

Really it's who I wanted to be…rich, famous, and lacking nothing.

Really it's who I wanted to become…stable, sustained, and knowing what is now and what is to come.

My desire is to know…

To know what to do to end this confusion.

To know how to go… to awaken my dying soul.

I need to know what to do. How do I go?

Is this the life you intended?

Why is that you don't answer me?

I see a reflection of the me that I am and the me I used to be and she is lifeless.

Who is she really supposed to be?

I AM BLACK WOMAN

Black Woman, yes that's me.

I am a Proud Nubian Queen.

I am the source from which all blackness flows.

My children are all shades and hues.

I am the Queen of Nile

    The Darkest Night

        The Star in the African Sky.

I am the Past, Present, and Future.

I am Black Woman – All of me!

I am Black People – All of them!

I am the womb from which Colin received his Powell

    And Condoleezza her Rice.

I am Beautifully Strong,

    Wonderfully Gifted,

        &

    Lovingly Kind.

I am ready for this world and the next

I am the source of beauty, strength and love.

I am the uniqueness you search for,

    The lips you pay for,

        And

The hips you pray for.

Who am I?

I am the True Black Woman!

WHAT DO YOU SEE WHEN YOU LOOK AT ME?

Do you see my heart, which has had pain unspeakable and joy incomprehensible?

Do you see my soul, open to living and not dying?

Do you see the shell I have tried to sustain to hide the truth?

Do you see the scars— the wounds of an adulterated past.

Do you see the wrinkles on my soul's face from the lies my mind has told my body.

Do you see the wisdom that grows deeper, rooting itself like a tree within me?

Do you see my heartache?

    My pain,

        My joy,

            My happiness,

                My revelation?

Do you see the healing that your smile has caused?

Do you see the happiness that is building within my soul?

Do you see the heart that your love has changed?

Do you see the confidence that has come back to me?

Do you see that I have overcome all that I've been through?

What is that you see when you look at me?

When I look in the mirror, I see the me I have become: A Queen Refined.

THIS IS FORCED

This writing is forced. Hell, sometimes this life is forced.

I'm forced to make decisions I'll hate.

I'm forced to deal with the issue of my weight.

I'd rather be me, but I'm forced to feel fat because society thinks that.

I'd rather be in love, but I am forced to feel less than secure when you are standing at my door.

This is forced!

This life is forced!

I'd rather be flying around the world, but I'm forced to work.

I'd rather spend my paycheck on happiness, but I'm forced to pay my life to a man for a roof, cable, and a phone.

Hell, I think I'd rather live alone.

This is forced!

This life, yeah, it's forced…I am forced to be a diva when I'd rather be a Queen.

Forced to be a B$%ch when I'd rather not be mean.

Forced to give you a piece of my mind when I'd rather be improving your way of thinking.

I'm forced to be in the world outside my window when I'd rather at home with you lying on my pillow.

IN HIS SERVICE

One of the most consistently evolving relationships in my life has been my relationship with God. He sees me ~ the beauty and even the mess. He sees the me He wants me to be. It's funny, I had other plans for my life but God's plans are always perfect and He will never fail. These poems were the very first love letters to Him.

DIFFERENT ME

When I am with you, I look different.

When I am with you, I talk different.

When I am with you, I act different.

    Could it be because you sustain me?

        Might it be that you rearranged me?

            Perhaps it is that you love me like no other.

Now that I am here and you are there, there is something in me that yearns for you,

    Something in me that desires you,

        Something in me that desires to speak to you.

My Soul is seeking you out, longing to have us together again.

When I am without you, I look different.

When I am without you, I act different.

When I am without you, I am different.

When I am without you, I realize

    Just how much I need you.

How much I yearn just to hear you whisper in my ear.

How much I long to call upon you and have you answer,

Yet I sit here wasting away – alone – without you.

You sit waiting for me to come back but my pride stands

in the way.

    I stand here wondering— is it possible to go back where we once where?

You sit looking as if to assure me –"Come to me!"

    I stand here unsure; not wanting to leave so many other things behind.

You smile,

    I race forward.

You reach out,

    I fall at your feet.

You embrace me,

    I cry out to you.

You tell me, "I told you I'd never leave you nor forsake you. I told you I won't change."

    I weep…

Without you I am nothing, but with you and through you, I can do ALL Things.

RUNNING FOR MY LIFE

I'm running from my present and its disasters.

I'm running from my future— bleak and uncertain.

I'm running towards my past; the way life used to be.

I want it all back…

If I could turn life's clock back I'd have you here.

If I could maneuver my way, you'd be with me and not with him.

I know His place is better but you belong here.

I can't stop the chains by myself; I need you here.

I know His Place is a castle and mine is a shack, but I need you here in my love.

I'd rather you'd live and not die.

I'd rather you'd stay and not go.

I want it all back.

I want the peace of hearing your voice on my phone.

I want to unlock the door and see you on the other side.

I want to see you on the porch waiting for me when I come home.

I want you back.

I want it all back.

I want to stop running.

I want it all back.

THE CALL

I want to show you life.
Are you willing to see it?

I want to show you love inside and out.
Are you willing to feel it?

I want to show you peace.
Are you willing to have it?

I can show you the world without wars,
life without death, and make you healed without scars,

but would you accept the world I'd show
or would you reject me and say no?

I can give you keys to a kingdom and you could reign there with me, but would you commit yourself to this kingdom or would you surrender your throne and deny me?

I can give you riches beyond any that you'd ever think or know, but would you reject my gift as too good to be true or would you accept that this is truly my love for you?

I can offer you a life better and greater but there is a Price...

    The price is your life.

I can show you all of this if you'd surrender your life; not as death to flesh but as life to soul.

You could live and not die, but you'd have to give your

life.

You could live forever with me, but you'd have to accept what's right.

You could walk together with me, but you'd have to set down your past and pick up your future.

You could have a life more abundantly but you'd have to give your life…

Will you take my call or will you reject me?

THE WONDROUS ONE

He'd part the sea just for me.

He'd move the mountains to set me free.

He cashes the checks my mouth writes when I am in trouble.

He hides me when the hitmen are closing in,

    And He shields me when they are close.

He defends me when I am right,

    And He has my back strong when I'm wrong.

He puts His strength in my weakness and His healing into my pain.

He puts His joy in my sorrow;

    He even brightens my tomorrow.

He snatched me from the pit of Hell and set my eyes on the prize.

He took what was empty in me and made it full.

He stood in the gap when the shots were fired; He took the bullets meant for me.

He loved me just enough and it was never too much.

He took my heart and put in all that should have been.

He became my Muse, my Inspiration, and my Knight in Shining Amour.

When I asked Him if I could cater to Him,

    He said, "just love Me."

When I asked if He'd let me take some of the load,

    He said, "I'll bear it all because you called My Name."

When I thought He was like the rest, He proved He was different.

He will Love Me until the End, just because He Loved Me & I called His Name.

You see, He proved His love was better the day He gave His Life for me.

THE MANNER OF HIS LOVE

What manner of love do you have for me?

You saw my faults and you looked past them to reveal my needs.

As I walked this earth aimlessly, you stopped me and put me on the right path.

Then you came and died for me— died so that I would not have to.

Now I know what real love is.

It took a mass of my life to understand your love for me, but I see it now.

You sacrificed everything just to save me.

You saved me from the filth in myself and I thank you.

Now I am free from the suffering and I am clean from the poison.

Thank you will never be enough to repay the manner of your love for me.

FALLING IN LOVE WITH MY FATHER

Daddy, I am in love with you again.

You flew into my life like the Red Eye.

You came in right on time.

You loved me unconditionally and never wavered.

You came in and loved me right past my pain.

You searched past my faults and discovered the true me.

You made a place in the space of my soul and all men now know

That it is you whom I love.

I love you again like I loved you before.

I stand in awe of who you are and realize I am not worthy.

I kneel at your feet in worship for no other reason than to love you.

I spread my arms before you and kiss the essence of your presence.

I adore you— you are the Almighty God; the sword and shield of my life.

You kept me in your bosom, safe from harm;

You freed me from the me I used to be and

That is why I love you

A LOVE STORY

One day I wondered what my love would look like on paper so I wrote it down, put it in a frame and out of it more love became.

ADDICTED

Passionately make love to me.

Don't stop.

I want you in the worst way;

I need you to come and stay.

I am addicted—Addicted to the passion you insight in me,

    Addicted to the energy you press into me,

    Addicted to the warmth of you against me.

I need you.

I want you.

I can't live without you.

I am addicted to you

    Like crack to an addict

    Like liquor to an alcoholic

    Like air to my lungs.

I need you.

To hell with the drama and all the formalities;

    You are all I need.

I am addicted to you—

    What would you have me do?

I need you.

I want you.

Give me all that you have.

I am addicted to your lips—

    The way they hug mine.

I am addicted to your eyes—

    The way they pursue me.

You are my addiction—

    My one true fix.

Kiss me as I succumb to you,

Hold me as I embrace you,

And love me as I encompass you.

Become addicted to me as I am addicted to you.

TO MY LOVE...

I wish you could see the way I love you.

How everyone and everything disappears when you walk into a room.

I wish you could understand the depth of my feelings for you.

Since the day I saw your face, my life has changed—there is no one I want more than you.

There is no one I'd rather spend my life with.

You've changed me in ways that I could never fully explain.

Some say that there is no such thing as soulmates, but I know in my heart that I am yours and you are mine.

You walked into my life and every other person I had ever loved seemed less than perfect compared to you.

I want to spend all of my days loving you.

I want to be all the love you need.

I want to be with you in every way, every day.

I want to make beautiful babies with you.

I want to be everything you've ever needed and wanted.

You are all the love I need and I hope that my love is all that you need.

I want to be your everything.

You are the love of my life.

You complete me.

Today I vow to give you my all because you loved me.

THANK YOU FOR LOVING ME

Thank you for loving me.

Thank you for inspiring me.

You pulled me back from the brink of death.

You pushed me gently towards life.

You nurtured my gift, inspired my creativity, and loved me to my core.

You enhanced the best of me

And accepted the worst of me.

Your light directed my new path and brought me from darkness into light.

You are the inspiration on every page,

    The HIM behind every thought and line,

        You are the inspiration of me.

Thank you!

TO MY KING WITH LOVE

I love you beyond words, my King.

There is none like you.

There are none more worthy to sit on the throne of my heart.

I am in disbelief that someone as excellent as you still exists, but here you are, my King.

You have become my life, my hopes, my dreams, and my love.

Without you, I'd have nothing else to live for; there would be nothing left for me to be.

All I know is your love and I am in awe of it.

You love me so well that it scares me.

Your heart and soul speak to me— they scream out my name.

Your big brown eyes draw me near like a spell; your kiss possesses me.

I cannot possibly contain myself when it comes to you, my King; you have complete control over me…
Mind, Body, and Soul.

WILL YOU LOVE ME?

Will you love me in the morning when everything is new?

    Will you love me in the evening when it all seems old again?

Will you love me despite all the wrongs I've done

    And all the rights that I never got around to?

Will you love me when my body is thinner, slimmer and firmer?

Will you love me when my belly is as big as a basketball?

    When my feet are swollen and my breasts are tender from the growth of our child that moves within me?

Will you love me when my hair is in desperate need of a relaxer?

    When my face is filled with the lines of age, heartache, and heritage?

Will you be there for me when the unity of our people has become like another child who is in desperate need of a mother's touch?

Will you love me in my success and my failure?

Will you love me when all of our dreams have come true?

Will you love me with nothing but the clothes on my

back and the shoes on my feet?

Will you love me when this body of mine becomes old, wrinkled, and ragged, as does everything with time?

Will you love me when I no longer have the ability to speak the words "I love you?"

Will you love me tomorrow if the day never came and the night became a part of forever for you and me?

Will you love me when my soul has left my body and there are no more words for me to say to you?

Will you love me when I am mortally no more?

Will you continue to love me through the Halls of Death until we are brought together again in the Heavens?

Will you love me?

FOR MALACHI

My son, I have loved you since the womb, and as I watch you grow, I love you more.

Your smile, your laugh— they are all parts of me.

You are the best part of my soul; the best part of this life that I once thought was worth nothing.

You bring me joy everlasting,

    You give me unconditional love,

        You are my true sunshine.

My love for you is different from any I have ever experienced —

    It's pure

        It's joy

            It's happiness.

You are the best part of me.

    You are my greatest endeavor and my greatest success.

        I love you.

THE VOWS (FOR MY HUSBAND)

Today when I say, "I do" I mean, "I do" to you for the rest of my life.

"I do" to the way that your eyes connect with mine.

"I do" to the way you say my name.

"I do" to the love we share.

"I do" to the way we share every moment with each other.

"I do" to the friends we are and will always be.

"I do" to the good times, the bad times, the happy times and the sad times.

You are my greatest challenge…

My biggest project…

And the light at the end of my dark tunnel.

"I do" live to love you.

"I do" love you for life.

"I do" know that you are the only love I will ever need.

"I do" to you,

To us,

To the rest of our lives…together.

THE EVOLUTION OF QUEEN

Oh, my Queen, your evolution has led us here.

We are together on this special day and I know again why it is that I love you.

It is your spirit— splendid and kind.

It is your drive to make it beyond what those before you achieved.

It is your womanhood— sleek and elegant, assertive yet gentle.

You are the passionate peace I searched for.

I will never see another woman as I see you.

You are...

My lover

My partner

My confidant

My joy

My day

My night

My every waking thought and every sleeping dream.

You are the serenity that I have so desperately longed for.

Although we have come so far apart, together we spring forth a new era in love.

The era in which our togetherness develops passion and love.

My Queen, your evolution of being continues and I know why you are Queen.

You are all that I have desired from a woman.

You are my forever love— gracious and humble, loving and kind, with so much to offer this King.

My Queen, I know why you are what you are— your evolution has opened up my eyes wider to you.

Now I know without a doubt that you are worthy of my love and I am worthy of yours.

I know that despite everything you are a Queen in every right and I shall love you forever as such.

SOME DAYS

There are some days when I know that you care,

Other days when I know you're there,

Other days when I wonder where I stand,

And days when I wonder how this might all end.

You came to me beautiful, loving, and caring.

    You have become a mystery, leaving me to wonder so much about you.

Some days are better…

        More affection

           More caring

              More romance.

Some days where I wish you were here…

    And days when I cannot wait to have your arms around me.

Then there are days when all of me needs all of you and I feel like I'm lost in a raging sea.

    And days when the sound of your voice is not enough to quench my longing.

And days when I have so much to say yet I feel it necessary to hold back.

    Days when I want to tell you everything yet only end up saying nothing really.

Days when I feel that there is nothing here but indiscretion.

    Times when hearing your voice makes my day.

Days when my life needs a friend and you seem not to be one.

    I came to you beautifully independent, whole and wonderfully made— exquisitely given, not searching yet somehow found.

    I have become what I thought I could never be: Satisfied, somewhat, with the idea of you and me.

Days when my soul longs to be touched

    And days when my heart desires to be kept.

Days when your laugh suppresses me and your voice sustains me.

    Days when I know what I see in you is so right.

Yet days when I am uncertain about who or what I want.

    Days when it becomes necessary to back away and let you just be you.

And days when I just need to hear you call me sweetie.

    Days when I'm diggin' you like hot chocolate & whipped cream.

Days when I feel that I'm in need of time & space. Some days I want to say everything but I really just don't know how.

YOUR TOUCH IS ALL I NEED

You touch me and I can breathe

You feel me and I can live

You love me and I am free

You envelop me and we become one.

You changed me…

    My walk

    My talk

    My step

    My in

    My out.

You rearranged me…

    My life

    My world

    My circumstances.

You saw me standing on my own and you stood by me.

You saw me on the brink of disaster and you saved me.

Even when I could not speak the words, you knew what was in my heart.

Oh, how your love has washed me, gently cleansing away all the others who soiled my heart.

Investing in me, wiping me clean and presenting me flawless— this is you.

You've given me joy like none other.

You've supplied all my needs great and small.

I am drawn to you…

    I long for you…Your touch is all I need.

AS LONG AS I AM QUEEN

As long as there are emotions in the ocean of my heart, I will long for you.

As long as the waves of the sea keep going, I will long for you.

As long as the tides keep flowing, I will long for you.

As long as the birds keep singing, I will long for you.

As long as my body has breath, I will long for you.

As long as the sun, the moon, and the stars shine, I will long for you.

As long as there is love in my heart, joy in my soul, and lust on my mind, I will long for you.

When day turns night and night turns day, I will be longing for you.

I will long for you until the world comes tumbling down around you and me, and we are left alone in the clouds.

YES, I DO LOVE YOU

I love you for who you are

    For who you were

        And for who you are becoming.

I love you for teaching me

    For choosing me

        For being the all to me.

I love you for supporting me

    For sheltering me

        For strengthening me.

You are my one true love

    My hero

        My God send.

You are the mate of my soul

    And the lover of my heart.

You are the antique jewel in my collection—

    My rare gem

        My succulent sapphire.

You are my all—

Lover of my heart,

Yes, I do love you.

LOVE SOUP

I made soup for us today and you were the main ingredient.

I put in my time,

    For time is the foundation of any relationship.

I put in all of my trust—

    The sealant for all good things.

I put in all my heart—

    The basis of my love begins here.

I put in my support of all you do—

    To let you know that I will always have your back and your front.

I added my friendship

    Because true love starts with true friendship.

Once all the ingredients were in, I let the love stew brew.

After maturing and fostering, it will soon be ready to serve;

    It's a love soup for two.

TRUTH IS...

Truth be told, I don't want to be here.

I'd rather have my feet cuddled next to yours.

I'd rather have your arms wrapped around my waist.

I'd rather be lying lovingly next to you, having you hold me.

Truth be told, I don't want to live here.

I'd rather live in you,

    On you,

        And next to you.

Truth be told, I like you but I also love you.

I love you more than that friendly love;

I love you like a woman loves her man;

I love you like a wife loves her husband.

Truth be told, I'd rather be with you than without you.

I'm down with you;

I'd go all around the world with you.

Truth be told, I've had your back since day one.

I'll be your support, your ear, your guide.

I'll be what you need and what you want.

The truth is that I love you. I respect you, and I am so glad I met you.

FOR MY WEDDING DAY

I thought this day would never come.

Yet here I am about to walk down the aisle.

I always knew that he & I would be together this way.

I guess it's the way my heart fluttered at the sound of his name.

I guess it's the way no other man could stand and compare.

Through good and bad he was my rock, my solace, and my comforter.

I am his angel, his diva divine, and his best friend.

I knew this day would come for us.

I sometimes feel like I am losing myself in him,

Yet I know that I am gaining a love like no other.

He has become my best friend,

My total companion, and my truest love source.

He cherishes me as though there is no one else in the world.

He captured my heart and has loved me unconditionally.

So this day, I take him to be my lawfully wedded husband.

YOU SHOULD HAVE

You wrote me a letter today—

You said you wanted to do this and that,

And then you left and went on your way.

You said you wanted to touch me—

I say you should have.

You said you wanted to caress me—

I say you should have.

You said what about being "just friends"—

I said I'd always be to you what you are to me.

You said but you'd see me differently—

I said I'll always see the love you give me, the care you show me, and the happiness you bring me.

You said but my heart breaks, it hurts because of another.

I said I understand your hurt and I embrace it as I embrace you.

You said you wanted to hold me but you were afraid I'd

want more.

I said you are the more that I know is in store.

You said you wanted to stay but you had to go.

I said I understand your parting and I know that love will bring you back.

ONCE UPON A LOVE TIME

I never thought I'd love you this much

I never thought I'd miss you this much

I never thought I'd live life without you.

Once upon a time, you loved me and you cared for me.

Once upon a love time, you were my king— the lover of my Mind, Body, Spirit

Once upon a love time, you made my heart dance with the anticipation of seeing your face.

Once upon a love time, you were my King and I was your Queen; no one loved you greater and no one loved me better.

Tragic nights…horrible decisions…lasting pain

You left me, not for cause, but for the gates of a place without space.

Tears…tears…tears

I was alone without you; living a royal life without my King.

You left me for a better place.

You left my Queendom for a better Kingdom.

And my heart aches for you…

My soul longs for you…

I can't breathe without you.

Once upon a love time, I had you…now I need you.

Once upon a love time, you were King…now I am Queen. Alone.

Once upon a love time, you held me…now my soul longs for you.

Tragic nights…horrible decisions…lasting pain

Tears…tears…tears

Once upon a love time, you were my everything, now life must be lived without you.

THINKING OF YOU

During the hot and steamy days, I think of you.

During the breezy humid nights, I think of you.

When life is sweet, I think of you.

When life is bitter, I think of you.

Thinking of you is all I seem to do.

I see your face in my dreams.

I hear your voice in my ears.

I feel your heart beating against mine.

When it seems that no one else loves me,

I think of how much your love surrounds me.

I think of you when all seems to fail.

I think of you in my sprawling success.

I think of the love we share, and I know you will always be there.

During the hot July nights, I think of you.

During the cold December days, I think of you more.

IT MAKES NO GOOD SENSE

Is it just me, or are we in love?

Is it just me, or are we right for each other?

It makes no good sense to love you the way I do.

It makes no good sense to care for you like I do.

It makes no good sense to be as into you as I am.

Although it makes no good sense, I'm crazy about you.

JUST BETWEEN YOU AND ME

Just between you and me, I've always been attracted your brown skin and muscular build.

Just between you and me, I'd love to spend my time knowing you.

Just between you and me, I'm interested in your head and your heart.

I see your sexy smile and it moves me.

I see your handsome face and it graces me.

I see the care in your heart and it elevates me.

I see the sweetness of your spirit and it draws me to you.

No other man stands out in my heart.

No other man captivates my soul.

You are my love— truly and completely.

COLD NIGHTS

It's the cold nights in which my body longs to be next to yours.

It's the cold nights when I wish you were here to hold me near.

It's the cold nights when I dream of waking up in the morning lying in your arms.

It's the cold nights that make me want to feel your chest against my back.

It's the cold nights when I want to hear you whisper my name.

It's the cold nights when I want to feel your breath against my ear.

It's the cold nights when I want you here.

It's the coldest nights that make me miss you the most.

FOR MY LOVE

You are all of me.

You are my in and my out.

You are my beginning and my end.

You are my life and my forever love.

You are my once and my always.

You are my serenity in chaos.

You are my calm sea,

My white sand beach,

My bluest ocean,

    My brightest sun,

        And my sweetest breeze.

You are my Heaven and my Earth.

You are my balance,

    You are my ground,

        You are my stability.

You are the umbilical cord of my existence— we cannot be severed.

SWEET THANG…I ADORE YOU

You had the magic key to unlock my cold heart.

You turned your key and made my heart love again.

You took the pain from my past and kissed it away.

You took away the shield surrounding my heart and gave it new life.

I always knew you'd come, sweet thang.

You took my hand and taught me how to love you,

Now I feel more love than I ever knew.

Sometimes, I don't know how to act; it is an emotion my Soul had all but forgotten.

I had forgotten what it felt like to love someone, but you turned my love song on and its music is beautiful to me.

Sweet thang, I adore you.

WHY I LEFT JAZZ

You brought me joy with your bass guitar.

You brought my smile back with your tap.

You loved me with your impeccable whine.

Oh how I loved you, Jazz,

But then one day, R&B found me.

I turned from him at first not wanting to leave my first love.

But R&B swooned me. He beckoned me.

His smooth lyrics captivated me and soon I was in a love affair with R&B.

They were the two greatest loves of my life – Jazz and R&B.

I could not choose between them because I truly loved them indeed.

Then one day Hip-Hop came my way and his beats, oh, they made my soul move.

Jazz had come close;

    R&B had almost done it.

But Hip-Hop, he touched me orgasmically and would not let go.

He made me feel things I'd never known.

He made me feel like I was truly grown.

Hip-Hop took over my soul.

Hip-Hop stole my heart from R&B and he was the reason I left Jazz.

BEHOLDING THE BEAUTY

I've been checking you out all night and I must say that you are exceptionally fine.

I say that with honesty and respect to you, my King.

You are a lovely site for this Queen's eyes; your beauty is intriguingly wondrous to me.

All thanks be to the King and Queen who came together to create such a wonderful figure of manhood.

I am grateful that I had the chance to feast my eyes upon your exquisite beauty.

If my time were more abundant, I would feast on your beauty for hours, but time for me is little, so I must turn away and be on my way.

Be assured, however, that I will be back to feast upon your beauty, if only for a moment.

IT'S TRUE…I LOVE YOU

I can no longer hold in my feelings—

I'm feelin' you.

    You are special to me.

        Our friendship, it means everything.

With you is always where I want to be.

I know your life is busy and I understand that now;

I know your heart is hurting and I am here for you now.

I'm here when you call.

I'll be there to support you…to stand by your side.

    I've got your back.

It's true that I love you.

AND MY MIND WONDERS

My mind wonders: when your heartbreak is through, will you allow me to love you?

Even when I ask it not, my mind wonders if it's just my friendship you want.

Even when I disconnect my thoughts, my mind wonders if you're feelin' me like I'm feelin' you.

Even when I daydream about my new life, my mind wonders if you'll call me when the miles between us are many.

And my mind wonders if you'll still be knowing me when you've got Oprah calling.

> But then I know you...
>
>> You'd pick up the phone to see if I were home.
>>
>> You'd set up to appear as long as I were there.
>>
>> You'd want me there with thoughts to share.
>>
>> You'd want me to see that I'm never alone.

And my mind wonders: if your heart were healed, would I be the one you'd choose to love you?

And my mind wonders if you'll ever want to be more than friends with me.

And my mind wonders...

> It wonders about you and me.

MISSING YOU BUT NOT REALLY TRYING

Today, I saw your walk and I knew how much I missed you.

I know the choice I made was right, but I miss you still.

I know that my decision was best, but my heart is still in a state of unrest.

I chose to be free and not bound;

To not be lost, yet found.

You chose a different street and a new avenue.

You think I'm not true to you, but to be true to you, I must choose me.

I realized this morning that I still love you despite the nays of my mind.

I realized that despite that love, I choose to continue to free my soul and pray for yours.

Pray that someday you'll see the good woman that resides in me and how she tried to love you completely.

TO JOHNNY WALKER RED

Let me wrap my arms around you and whisper in your ear.

Let me make you understand exactly how I feel.

When I first looked at you, my heart never realized the depth of you.

When I took my first gaze into your eyes, I never realized how much you'd change me.

I'm not really sure when, but along the way, I fell for you.

I fell for your laugh— though each laugh for each mood is different, I can hear them even though you are miles away.

I fell for your soul; it's a good soul, a true and living soul that knows God.

I fell for all the things that made you different and distinctly you.

You showed me it was ok to be real.

You taught me to love without touch and to live freely without fear.

I esteem you highly as a friend and as my sweetheart.

I am in love with you— with all of you.

I am impressed by you and all that you do.

I am impressed by all of you.

EASIER SAID THAN DONE

I can't turn off the light that my life has paved for you.

You stepped into my world and changed me.

I do not want another in your place; there is no one who can fill your shoes.

It's easy to say just walk away but it's hard to do.

I don't choose to have you go, but I'll love you if you decide to leave.

You ask me to understand— after all, we are "just friends."

It's easier said than done, baby.

Tell your story to my heart…it's not listening to my reasoning.

I can't make it stop loving you.

I can't stop my heart from skipping beats when you are near.

It hurts when you are not here.

Loving you is not easier said than done. I do it sincerely.

DISTANT FRIEND

I had you on my mind today.

There was no rhyme or reason. Nothing I really thought to say.

But something about my day brought you to the forefront of my mind.

Not sure if it was a smell or a taste, but

      Something brought you to my thoughts
Although I am not sure what.

My mind thought of you today —

    It reminded me of your smile,

        And I heard you call me.

    It reminded me of your touch,

        And I felt you next to me.

    It reminded me of your scent,

        And I felt you hold me.

My mind wanted to see you today — not a still picture of You but the real you. The new you.

Can you see that I miss you?

Are my feelings obvious or are you just oblivious to me?

Can you see that I want you, not in a perverted way, but I seek to draw my nectar from the wisdom in your mind?

Can you see that it's love that drapes your face over my mind?

My mind longed for you today, not in a sexual way, but I seek to share intimacy with your mind.

I thought about you today…

My heart missed you today…

My Soul loved all of you today…

I am enchanted with you, my distant friend.

I LOVE YOU

I am in love with you,

Not the physical manifestation of you,

But I am in love with the man who resides inside you.

I am in love with you like a wife loves her husband.

Like Christ loves His Church.

Before I lay my head to sleep, it's you with whom I long to speak.

I pray that the Lord of my Soul would find a way to let you know that you're my mate.

My heart sings when I see it's your number on my caller ID.

I never want to be apart from you; I can't imagine living my life without you.

I could live a thousand lives as long as you were by my side.

You inspire me to do great things.

You challenge me to make tall moves.

Your soul is beautiful; your mind is wonderful…

I am in love with you…all of you.

VOICE OF THE QUEEN

I used to be militant and wanted desperately to be part of the Black Power movement not because of hate but because I saw something in the struggle. I saw that the voices of those in the movement made a difference and I wanted to be a change agent. As I matured, I realized that my voice could be heard without shadow of Black Power but rather through the heart of a Mother's love.

~ Liela

THE MOTHER IN ME

It's the mother in me that wants to embrace you.

It's the mother in me that wants to sit you here with my hands in your hair, discussing life's affairs.

It's the mother in me that wishes you'd never have to struggle like I did or like my mother did before me.

It's the mother in me that wants to hold you when you cry and never let you go.

I see so much of me in you;

>Your eyes are mine
>
>My nose is yours
>
>Your hair is mine
>
>My smile is yours.

The mother in me wants you to stay in my arms forever, but the Soul of me knows you must fly.

You are my priceless jewel in a flawless crown.

You are the epiphany of me—Mind, Body and Soul.

I HAVE TRIED TO SAVE YOU

Here I sit in this unsatisfied state, discussing the matters of your distress among the beings of Spirit, and I find myself crying.

I thought that I could save you from yourself. I have done everything I know how to do and you are still in danger.

I sit and wonder how long it will be before everything collapses around my people.

How long before we mentally overthrow our enemies who only have their best interest in mind?

How long before we take responsibility for our own actions and stop blaming "The Man"?

How long before we destroy what our ancestors worked so hard to build?

How many of our young people have to die for us to take a STAND?

How many children have to live without a father before we SPEAK UP?

We were once a STRONG people who STOOD for SOMETHING, but those that are STRONG and WILLING are few and have little voice against the ringing gun shots.

It's time to take back OURSELVES, OUR PRIDE, AND OUR FUTURE…ARE YOU READY TO STAND?

I SEE IN YOU

I wonder if you see what I see in you —

I see love in you

I see potential the world through

I see destiny in you.

You, the blossoming rose,

I see the perfection in your bud

I see purpose in your thorn and

Passion in your flower.

You, the unbalanced child, attempting the walk into genius —

You can possess the land…it's yours for the taking,

You can have the answer just by asking the right questions.

I wonder if you see the potential in your eyes.

I wonder if you can see the potential in your face.

If only you'd open your mind to what your heart already knows.

If only you'd let the real you become, then, precious one, you would see the you I already know.

WISHES AND DREAMS

I wish you love in the midst of sorrows.

I wish you light in the midst of darkness.

I wish you joy in the midst of heartache.

My wish for you far exceeds your dreams.

I wish you life without pain,
    Joy without rain, and
        Your love unchained.

I wish you determination, love, and redemption.

I wish you happy and rejoicing.

I wish you non-conforming—
    United together and lacking nothing.

I wish you'd see the all that I wish for you.

I wish you'd feel the joy I feel for you.

I wish you'd see the love I see for you.

I wish you'd see the world as true as you.

<u>FOR MY MOTHERS</u>

You are my inspiration

My desire

My success.

I counted on you when all else failed me.

You nurtured my spirit, my mind, and my body with the love only a momma can give.

I became the apple of your eye & you are the jewel of my heart.

The reason I strive is to make you smile.

The reason I pray is because you showed the way.

The reason I love is because you always loved me.

I am the apple of your eye and you are my special jewel.

SISTER 2 SISTER

I have watched you since birth;

I watched you grow.

Now you think you know—

You think you've got it all together.

You have your mind sewn around nothing,

Wandering aimlessly, thinking you're going everywhere—

Jumping from place to place and face to face,

Trying to do everything but really doing nothing.

You're wondering when your time will come:

It's already here, yet you can't see it.

I wish so much for you but my wish will never make you.

When I look into your eyes, I see the real you.

I see the sadness life has brought you.

When I try to speak, love holds me back.

When I try to tell you right, love covers my lips.

When I try to step in and carry you, love steps in and denies me.

Momma always said, "You can take a horse to the water, but you can't make him drink."

When I want to tell you are making deadly mistakes,

    Love says, "no, she'll grow."

When I want to advise you in life matters,

    Love says, "no, let her get her wings."

As I sit with the elders contemplating your fate, I wonder if Love was right.

I wonder if I should tell you that life is more than you're making it.

I wonder if Love is right.

I remember your face as I said, "take it slow, boo. Don't rush life or you might lose it."

I remember your voice saying, "I'm grown now, I can handle it. Nobody knows what I am doing. It's not what you think."

You thought you had it all, yet when life got real, you looked to me.

You thought you could handle all life had to give but when the giving was too much, you asked me to help you receive.

I have answers but are you ready to listen and not just hear?

You said you need my advice because now life was deep, your plans weren't working and you were afraid.

Sister 2 Sister, you need me.

Sister 2 Sister, I need you.

Lean on me…let me be your backbone and your advice column.

Sister 2 Sister…we need each other.

I REMEMBER WHO YOU USED TO BE (FOR CAMDEN, NJ)

I remember when you were lovely, strong, and righteous.

I remember when you cared for me and I cared for you.

I remember your beauty, as eternal as heaven.

I remember your love, as hopeful as the Resurrection.

I remember you when you were the "it" place to be.

I remember when I first met you;

You were shy at first

But then you showed me your true beauty.

Your smile shined brightly.

Your walk embraced me.

You loved me in your way.

You proved me wrong and made me see your beautiful right.

You cared for your children;

You knew them by name.

You knew the good and the bad, the in and the out, the ugly and the pretty.

Even when you did not like their choices, you accepted your children.

You had a passion for peace and a longing for love.

I miss my old-school ghetto— how it taught me.

It took me, young and pure, and it showed me how people could live if they only just loved.

It showed me pride. Pride in my skin, my shape and my history.

It showed me love for all— from neighbor to neighbor and friend to friend.

I trusted my life with you and you trusted your life with me.

One always knew another and life was not always fair, but we loved good anyway.

Sometimes "Good Times" was more like my real life than TV life.

I miss what I used to be when we were moving on up, and now we're stuck in a rut not knowing which door will let us out.

What happened to the old-school ghetto that I loved so much?

FROM THE AUTHOR

Thank you for taking this journey with me. Each poem is a reflection of my life - the good, the bad, the ugly and the indifferent. I am often asked if everything I've written about has happened to me and the answer is each poem is a reflection of my life. Sometimes in life you are a witness and sometimes you are the participant. We don't always get to choose what we see, hear, feel, experience or go through but we can choose how we respond. My response is often writing and creating. So the journey you have just taken has been a part of the glorious process of my life. It is my hope that you enjoyed the journey and that you will share your thoughts with me and with others by reviewing this book or emailing me at lielamfuller@jadoraschild.com.

Thank you again!

Liela

Upcoming Titles From Jadora's Child Publishing

Poured from a Broken Vessel
Shanean Paige Saylor

Love Letters of a Worshipper
Liela Marie Fuller

Be sure to visit our website – www.jadoraschild.com - for more details and to follow all of our authors. Follow us on Facebook (https://www.facebook.com/jadoraschildpublishing) and Twitter (@authorljmarie)

About the Author

Liela Marie Fuller is an Author, Poet, and Founder of Jadora's Child Publishing. Over the years, she has written countless poems, short stories and articles on everything from love to politics. Her editorial writings have been published in the Hartford Courant newspaper Liela founded Jadora's Child Publishing in 2014 to help these writers become successful authors.

In addition to being the founder and CEO of Jadora's Child Publishing, Liela is also working on 3 new books to be published in 2015.

Liela is also the founder of Heavenly Help Computer Solutions and MERK Media.

Liela was born and raised in Camden, NJ and is the proud Mother of one son and Auntie of three nieces and two nephews. Liela is also an avid reader, car enthusiast, and coffee connoisseur! When Liela is not writing, she enjoys spending quality time with family and friends.

www.ingramcontent.com/pod-product-compliance
Lightning Source LLC
Chambersburg PA
CBHW020912090426
42736CB00008B/593